D0591894

NEW GUIDE TO
CAPRI

Editions KINA ITALIA

INTRODUCTION

Capros (i.e. wild boar, for its characteristic shape) to the ancient Greek colonists, *Capraea and Insula Sirenussae* (i.e. bitter, rocky island and mermaids' island) to the Latins, *Antheomoessa* (i.e. Land in flower) to Homer, *Apragopolis* (i.e. land of sweet idleness) to Emperor Augustus: these names and nicknames, conjuring up bitterness and sweetness at the same time, assi-

gned to the island of Capri over the centuries are probably enough to describe the various aspects of this land of matchless beauty and enchantment.

The island, which is quite small (its perimeter is no longer than 17 km), is almost completely formed by limestone rock which, during the course of the millenniums, the elements and geological movements have modelled into mountainous reliefs (the highest peak, Monte Solaro, reaches an altitude of 589 m); they drop more gently down into a series of rolling hills and two large plateaus divided

An enchanting view of Capri at sunset

at the neck of the island, between Marina Grande and Marina Piccola, which in turn drop down to the sea often in the form of steep, jagged cliffs indented in small creeks, caves and ravines, or projecting in mini peninsulas and headlands that offer unforgettable panoramas, or even adorned with rocks or gigantic masses that emerge majestically from the water. On this land, the vegetation has grown in line with the climate, always mild and quite dry, colouring the rock green with woods and spontaneous vegetation, low and thick, or with the lively colours of its numerous flowers, colours which have been enriched over the course of the centuries with those of grapes, olive trees and citrus fruit plantations cultivated by man in the more fertile areas. A perfect natural environment (which is today actively protected) for numerous animal species, living both on the land and in the water, common or rare like the *Podarcis sicula coerulea*, the famous blue lizard that only lives on one of the island's Faraglioni rocks. Capri, the *paradise of idleness*, to call it as Emperor Augustus did, i.e. away from the pressures of daily working life, to be dedicated to the discovery of nature and the many historical and artistic beauties of the island: the deep sea, the matchless panoramas, the picturesque villages, the ruins of ancient Roman villas, the Charterhouse and the churches, the castles, the palaces, the countless private villas, the towers, the caves... These are probably the mermaids that figure in the legends which, with their melodious and irresistible charm attracted onto the island not only two emperors but also a large number of painters, writers, musicians, scholars and artists who found inspiration for their works or simply wished to pay homage to Capri, "Reina de roca, en tu vestido de amaranto y azucena", (Queen of Rock, in your cockscomb and white lily robe), as Pablo Naruda wrote.

A characteristic view

HISTORY

The presence of man on Capri during prehistorical times has been proved by finds including weapons and tools of various kinds and tombs dating back to a period between the Palaeolithic and the Bronze Age in many places on the island, including the Valley of Tragara and Grotta delle Felci. Little is known about the island's first inhabitants. Capri was mentioned by Virgil in the *Aeneid*, in which the name of Telone, king of the Teleboi, appears, but it is not historically proved that this people actually colonized the island. The Phoenicians and Etruscans certainly frequented it but did

not settle there. It is quite plausible that the first colonizers were the Cumaeans, the Greeks who settled in the gulf of Naples and surrounding areas. Remains of the Greek period include the ruins of the town walls and probably also those of the Phoenician Steps. In the 5th and 4th centuries BC, when it passed under the rule of Naples, the island took on considerable importance both for its strategic position (from a commercial and military viewpoint) and its flourishing forms of art and culture.

In 328 BC, Naples submitted to the Romans and Capri also passed under their control. It was, however, almost ignored until 29 BC, when it was discovered by Octavianus (later Augustus), who fell in love with it, managed to take it over from Naples in exchange for Ischia

A plan of the island made of majolica

and frequented it until his death (14 A.D.). His successor Tiberius was equally enchanted by the beauty of the island and lived there for over ten years. Capri thus lived a period of great splendour: it became the site not only of magnificent villas but also of great civil engineering projects such as berths, wharves, tanks, roads and lighthouses. After Tiberus' death (37 AD), the constructions were abandoned and many fell into ruin.The early centuries of the Middle Ages were marked for Capri, which had

become solely a fisherman's island, by the threat of raids first by the Vandals and later by the Saracens. After the 10th century the island passed into the hands of the Normans, the Swabians and then the Angevins: when governed by Naples (until 1443 the capital of the Kingdom of

A charming picture of the island

Sicily), it enjoyed a period of relative tranquillity, due in part to the concessions made by Charles II and Joan I (under whose reign the Charterhouse of St. James was founded), which had positive repercussions on its economic and social aspects. Having succeeded the Angevins, the Aragonese maintained the privileges that the island already enjoyed.In the 16th century, the island was the scene of raids by the Turks, led by the pirate Frederick Barbarossa, who took it by assault several times causing destruction and death. Further mourning was caused in 1856 by the plague. The Bourbon's rule in the 18th century was characterized by two main aspects: the concession of various privileges, required in order to overcome the extreme poverty caused by bad government and

the removal of many archaeological treasures discovered on the island during the excavations carried out above all by the order of Ferdinand IV. In January 1806, Napoleon's troops conquered Naples and set up a military garrison on Capri to contrast attacks by the English who had become the Bourbons' allies. In May 1806, the English actually landed on Capri, defeated the French and set up a military government on the island. But in October 1808 the French, by order of Joachim Murat (who had come to the throne of the Kingdom of Naples) won back Capri after a violent battle. The island's appearance underwent considerable changes during this period and until the Bourbons returned to power in 1815, above all due to the massive construction of fortifications, while the popu-

A panorama from the air

lation lived a period of severe poverty from which it only began to recover later on, in part due to tourism which appeared as early as the 19th century and began to play a decisive role after the second world war, when the island was made a *rest camp* of the United States army. Frequented by the ilite (artists, intellectuals and scientists) until the middle of the present century, it has become increasingly a target for the masses, representing, in some cases, a serious threat to the safeguarding of the island's natural and artistic beauties, to the protection of which today various institutions are dedicated.

MARINA GRANDE

Situated on the Northern coast at the point in which the island narrows into its characteristic "bottleneck", Marina Grande is the main port of Capri, the mooring place for ferries from Naples and Sorrento and the tourist boats that take visitors to Grotta Azzurra or around the island. The port was built in 1928 under the shelter of a long wharf and occupies a section of the beach (a free part and a part occupied by bathing esta-

blishments) which runs along the entire inlet in which the town has developed. It is the island's third biggest town, in size and number of inhabitants, after Capri and Anacapri and, due to its excellent facilities, it is much frequented by tourists particularly during the summer and is the classical departure point for trips and visits to the various points of naturalistic and cultural interest on the island. In the immediate vicinity of Marina Grande stands the little that remains of Emperor Augustus' Seaside Palace and, down below, the majestic ruins of Tiberius' Baths (belonging to Augustus' villa).The archaeological area can be reached on foot by following a short path (via the Seaside Palace) along which you come across some beautiful villas containing valuable items from the Seaside Palace

The port of Marina Grande with Monte Solaro in the background

excavations. Near the port, in Piazza della Vittoria, there is the bottom station of the funicular railway which takes the shortest route to the panoramic terrace of the town of Capri. You can walk up the same way to enjoy wonderful views and the panorama of the island offered by the various roads that climb up throgh the vegetation to the town. Going up via Colombo you enter, after a short while, via Marina Grande, lined by villas, gardens and hotels, some of which stand on archaeological sites where important Roman ruins have been discovered (a sarcophagus, a marble altar and some small statues). Almost immediately afterwards, you come to the start of the Phoenician Steps, which lead all the way up to Anacapri. Extremely close by stands the church of St. Constant or "Madonna della Libera" built on the site of ruins from Roman times, around the 8th century. Modified during the 10th and 11th centuries and then, by order of Count Giacomo Arcucci, in the 14th century. It conserves in its interior, four columns and some precious marble works coming from one of the imperial

The bathing establishment and port of Marina Grande

Marina Grande by night

villas on the island. Dedicated in ancient times to the patron saint of Capri (the patriarch of Constantinople, St. Constant), it is visited every year, on 14th May, by a solemn procession of fishermen who carry here, from the church of St. Stephen in Capri, the silver bust of the saint, which is taken back to Capri a few days later. Continuing further on, the road offers breathtaking views of Marina Grande, Capri and the road that leads from Capri to Anacapri; in the vicinity of the top station of the funicular railway, you pass beside the two cemeteries of Capri, the Catholic cemetery (1875) and, in the thick vegetation, the non-Catholic cemetery, set up in 1878 by the Capri doctor Ignazio Cerio to ensure a worthy burial for those who did not follow the religion of the Roman Catholic Church.

As an alternative to this route, you can take the panoramic road of St. Francis, which bears this name due to the presence in the vicinity of a small fort built at the start of the 19th century by the French on the site of a pre-existent monastery dedicated to the saint. The road, which leads up steps to the Piazzetta (Piazza Umberto I) of Capri, is entered having gone all the way along via Ruocco from the port. A last alternative for reaching Capri, a shorter but steeper route, is via Truglio which follows the

Another view of the port of Marina Grande seen from above

path of the funicular railway for a while and climbs up to meet via Acquaviva, which leads into the Piazzetta. In the area around via Truglio remarkable finds from imperial times have been brought to light, the most outstanding of which is a statue of Tiberius currently exhibited at the Louvre.

Picturesque view of Marina Grande

THE SEASIDE PALACE

This name indicates the site of the favourite seaside villa of Augustus, who had it built in the area currently occupied by Marina Grande on the basis of the traditional architectural principles of this type of buildings. Almost certainly designed by the great court architect Masgaba, who was behind many works on the island, the palace stretched across a vast surface area dropping down in a series of terraces down to the sea and was, in all probability, formed by a residential section consisting of small rooms and small independent buildings and a bathing section linked to the previous part by steps, with nymphaeums, baths, a small landing-place and tanks for fish-breeding. Inland there were large tanks for collecting water. The palace must have been surrounded by gardens that extended as far as the area currently occupied by the sports ground. While there remain impressive ruins of the bathing section of the villa, Tiberius' Baths, hardly anything remains of the residential section. A large part of the responsibility for the scarcity of the remains may be attributed to Norbert Hadrawa, the merchant who, between the end of the 18th century and the start of the 19th century, with the authorization of King Ferdinand of Bourbon, removed something like 14 tons of ancient marble and works which were, in part, kept as precious finds, in part, used as construction material and, in part, even ground to obtain lime. Some of the destruction was even caused by the English and French troops who, at the start of the 19th century, razed to the ground the area on which the gardens stood in order to create a parade ground for military purposes.

Typical Capri architecture

TIBERIUS' BATHS

This is the name given to the ruins of what must have been the bathing area of Augustus' grand villa. Studies conducted on the ruins suggest that the complex, built in Augustus' time and probably modernized or expanded during the rule of his successor Tiberius, consisted of impressive walls built in *"opus reticulatum"* terminating in an exedra-nymphaeum, with walls completely covered with precious marble, adorned with a colonnade and linked to the beach by a flight of steps, a small port and tanks used for breeding fish and shellfish. Of the original installation, up to the present

day there remain traces of the exedra and great walls, the landingplace and the swimming pools, in addition to many finds which were fortunately left behind by Hadrawa and are currently exhibited in museums. Depending on the fish bred, some of these tanks contained salt water, while others were supplied with fresh water from a special aqueduct. To change the water and ensure that it was always clean, all tanks were directly connected to the sea by a complex pipe system.

The impressive ruins of Tiberius' Baths

THE FUNICULAR RAILWAY

Built in 1907, it sets off from Marina Grande and, in five minutes, covers a distance of about 650 m permitting passengers to enjoy some spectacular views of the island, to the famous Piazzetta (Piazza Umberto I). At its point of arrival (138 m above sea level) opens out the terrace of the funicular railway, which the writer Alberto Savinio defined "[...] the anteroom of Capri, [...], a sampling room open to the four winds, providing a small but sure sample of all the delights offered by the island of goats." In fact, the terrace dominates the Gulf of Naples (on a clear day you can also see Ischia, Procida and Vivara), Marina Grande, the foot of Monte Solaro (the island's highest peak, at 589 m) and the surrounding panorama scattered with villas, orchards and gardens. The houses that stand to the east of the terrace have covered, over the years, what remained of the ancient Greek and Medieval walls, today almost completely hidden.

The "Loggetta", a belvedere

A beautiful view of the funicular railway

LA PIAZZETTA

Piazza Umberto I, as it is referred to officially, is exactly what the islanders and tourists call it: a "piazzetta" (small square). It is the heart of the town and can be reached from the terrace of the funicular railway or by passing through its ancient Medieval entrance. The square is delimited by the town hall, the steps that lead to the Church of St. Stephen and the impressive Clock Tower. On the façade of the town hall (the building dates back to the 14th century) there are two plaques in memory of Victor Emanuel II and Umbert I, while its internal courtyard houses some finds from Roman times discovered on the island. The Clock Tower is also known as the "campanile della Piazzetta" (the square's bell tower): in fact, while some believe that it is one of the many watch towers on the island, others believe that it is a modified version of the bell tower of the pre-existent church of St. Sophia, destroyed in the 17th century. But what makes this "Piazzetta" one of the most famous places on Capri is not so much these monu-

Piazza Umberto I, the famous "Piazzetta"

ments, the façades of the characteristic architecture and small shops that surround it but the special mixed atmosphere of the worldly and everyday life that can be felt among the tables of the cafis, where you can meet tourists and artists, common people and the great names of show business and culture, all attracted by the simple, clean beauty of this small permanently crowded area. Until the second half of the Thirties, the few existing bars did not have tables outdoors: this novelty was introduced by the Gran Caffh Vuotto and it was from this moment on that the Piazzetta became "the" meeting place par excellence in the whole of Capri.

The "Piazzetta":
The characteristic cafis
and shops

The oriental dome of
the church of St.
Stephen

The clock tower, also
known as the
"Campanile della
Piazzetta"

An attractive view by
night

THE CHURCH OF ST. STEPHEN

It is the island's largest church and was a cathedral until 1818, the year in which the diocese of Capri was incorporated in the Sorrento diocese. The building was designed by Francesco Antonio Picchiatti and then built, probably on the site of the ancient church of St. Sophia, by Marziale Desiderio from Amalfi during the last decade of the 17th century. The external architecture of the church, bright white with a baroque façade, is remarkable above all for the oriental motif created by the central dome and the vaults of the side chapels. Its interior with three aisles flanked by chapels, is enriched with marble taken from Roman buildings and interesting paintings. To the left of the presbytery stands the silver statue of St. Constant, the patriarch of Constantinople and the island's patron saint.

The white façade of the church of St. Stephen

PALAZZO CERIO

The palace, which has rather a stern and massive appearance, is situated in the square of the same name opposite the church of St. Stephen. It owes its current name to the fact that it houses a Capri study centre named after the doctor Ignazio Cerio, father of the island's most famous scholars, Edwin. In reality, it was built in the 14th century by order of the Arcucci family, the noble and wealthy family of Giacomo Arcucci, founder of the Charterhouse of Capri and secretary of Queen Joan I of Anjou, who lived in the palace for a certain period of time. Modernized towards the end of the 17th century and expanded in the 19th century, it was also used over the years as an orphanage and as a hotel before housing the current institution.

The steps and entrance to Palazzo Cerio

THE CHARTERHOUSE OF ST. JAMES

A remarkable example of Medieval architecture, the Charterhouse dedicated to the apostle James stands at a short distance from the centre of Capri in an area, in part, cultivated with olive trees and vine and, in part, occupied by recent buildings that create a certain contrast with its 14th century style. The construction of the great monastic complex, build by order of Count Giacomo Arcucci, the secretary and treasurer of Queen Joan I of Anjou, began around 1363 and was then resumed between 1371 and 1374. The early centuries of the monastery's history, like that of the whole island, were marked by the devastating raids by Ottoman pirates, like the raid of 1553 in which it was sacked and set on fire by the pirate Dragut or the one that took place eleven years later, which made the Carthusians decide to build a tower of defence on its Southern side, which collapsed in 1808. During the same year, Napoleon's government ordered the suppression of the Charterhouse, the annulment of its many privileges (which had,

The Major Cloisters of the Charterhouse

in some periods, been the cause of considerable protest by the island's population), the confiscation of all its assets and the expulsion of all the monks from the island. Having been used for housing the troops, in 1815 the complex was employed by the Bourbons as a prison and later as a home for veteran or invalid soldiers and, finally, from 1860 till the start of the 20th century, as a place of confinement for soldiers guilty of indiscipline or more serious offences. In the early years of the century, the Charterhouse risked passing into the hands of a company that intended to convert it into a hotel complex and escaped this fate as a result of the intervention of Benedetto Croce, being entrusted first to the Ministry of Education and later to the Ministry for Arts and Culture. In 1927 a restoration project was undertaken to return the ancient buildings to their splendour. Further work was carried out at the end of the Eighties.

A visit to the Charterhouse enables you to observe, around the primitive Medieval complex, the outcome of the various restoration projects (the first was undertaken immediately after Dragut's

A characteristic detail of the Minor Cloisters of the Charterhouse

raid in 1553), modifications and additions that succeeded one another over the centuries. Following the avenue leading to the monastery along which is situated the building once occupied by the monastery's chemists' laboratory and the Women's Chapel, you come to the church of St. James (beside the entrance to the Charterhouse). The ogival portal, the lunette of which is crowned by a 14th century fresco depicting the Virgin Mary and the Child between Saints Bruno and James, beside which appear Queen Joan I and Count Arcucci, gives access to its austere single-aisle interior (restored in 1927), with elegant cross vaults and 17th and 18th century frescos. From the tower that stands beside the church you enter the Charterhouse itself, part of

which is occupied by the buildings dedicated to the monks' daily activities (the monks' cells, warehouses, stables and rooms for entertaining visitors and pilgrims who did not belong to the Carthusian order). The largest part is occupied by the convent of seclusion, formed by cloisters (the minor 14th century cloisters, modified during the following century and the major cloisters dating back to the end of the 16th century), the gallery, the refectory, the chapter-house, the fathers' cells, the prior's apartment and the Clock Tower (both of the latter were added during the 17th century). The refectory area and the gallery area that was used for connecting the two cloisters has housed, since 1974, the museum dedicated to Karl

The magnificent architectural complex of the Charterhouse among olive trees and vineyards

Wilhelm Dieffenbach, which conserves numerous works (including some original views of Capri such as *"Marina Piccola" and "Le Grotte Marine" (the Seaside Caves)* by the controversial German painter who lived on Capri between the 19th and 20th centuries. In an adjacent room, you can admire valuable archaeological finds, an altar and two Roman marble statues brought to light in 1964 during research work carried out on the water in Grotta Azzurra: ruined to a considerable extent by the corrosive action of the water and salt, one represents a triton and the other the God Poseidon. The minor cloisters, enclosed by an elegant portico with 15th century round arches supported by pillars dating back to Roman times adorned with capitals, in part Roman and in part Byzantine, are contrasted by the adjacent Clock Tower in baroque style. Round arches, resting on larger pillars. They also frame the major cloisters on which the cells of the Carthusian fathers' cells overlooked: some of these now house the "Virgilio

Another beautiful picture of the Major Cloisters of the Charterhouse

Marone" secondary school, the chapter-house and other rooms. Below the cloisters stands a large tank constituting the water supply for the complex which has a remarkable lunette vault. On the righthand side of the cloisters, added in the 17th century and not part of the classical design of Carthusian monasteries, is situated the prior's apartment and annexed garden, today a lookout from which you get a magnificent view of the sea, the Faraglioni and Punta Tragara.

Head of a statue from Roman times found in Grotta Azzurra

The beautiful public gardens, situated at a point sheer above the sea at a short distance from the Charterhouse of St. James, were set up at the start of the century by Friedrich August Krupp, an extremely rich German industrialist who lived between the 19th and 20th centuries. The terraces, set in a luxuriant vegetation formed by various kinds of trees and brightly-coloured flowerbeds in bloom and adorned with beautiful statues (at the bottom of the area with the children's playground, there is also a stele by Giacomo Manzù dedicated to Lenin, who was on Capri at the start of the century), were constructed in the Thirties when, Mr. Krupp having died many years earlier, the gardens were expropriated from the Commune and opened to the public. From the park you get a spectacular view of the town of Capri, the Faraglioni and Marina Piccola. The park was named after Emperor Augustus in 1918 for "political" reasons: immediately after the first world war, the Commune felt that it was better to avoid using a German name like Krupp.
Nicknamed the "King of cannons", Krupp

lived in Capri from 1898 to 1902, the year in which he died in Germany, and played a leading role both in the determining the appearance of some places on Capri (he was responsible, not only for this park, but also for the construction of the spectacular street that bears his name) and in the island's worldly affairs at the centre of which Krupp remained for a long period due to fact that he was accused of being a homosexual and indulging in libertine behaviour. Irrespective of whether these accusations were true or false, the rich industrialist showed a growing love for the land that had given him hospitality, not only by embellishing it with the works mentioned previously, but also by making a significant contribution to research on the local marine fauna. He donated two boats that he had had built specially for this purpose.

The luxuriant vegetation in Augustus' Gardens

Again it was Friedrich August Krupp behind the construction of this beautiful road that winds its way up, with its bold, spectacular bends dug into the rock sheer above the sea, fitting perfectly into the panorama and surrounding vegetation. The road, which is about 1350 m long, was designed by the engineer Emilio Mayer and built in 1901 on a large estate that Krupp had purchased in order to be able to construct a road that linked his villa to the nearby town of Capri. Now, via Krupp leads from Augustus' Gardens to Marina Piccola. Halfway along it there is a gateway, on the other side of which you come to Grotta di Fra' Felice, a cave that the German industrialist curiously decided to convert into a small residence on two floors to be used when meeting up with friends.

"Belvedere del Cannone" with the famous Faraglioni rocks in the background

The spectacular via Krupp

PUNTA TRAGARA

Situated at the east end of the island's southern shore, the headland projects out to the open sea in an exceptionally panoramic position. It is reached along the street of the same name which, starting from Capri, runs down a slight slope and opens out into a terrace, the Belvedere of Tragara, where you can admire, from close up, the Faraglioni rocks and the Rock of Monacone, the village of Marina Piccola resting at the foot of the valley of Tragara and the bathing area below, the slopes of Monte Solaro

in the background and the impressive wall of Monte Castiglione, of which you can identify the Medieval castle (9th-10th century) on the summit. From here you can walk down the road that leads first to another spectacular lookout sheer above the sea and then to the famous Grotta di Matromania, or take the enchanting road that leads to the small port of Tragara, framed by a small beach. The landing place, situated in a place of great natural beauty, was probably built during the period when the island was inhabited by the Roman emperors, as witnessed by the ruins of walls dating back to imperial times.

The Faraglioni rocks seen from Punta Tragara

The enchanting road to Tragara

CASA MALAPARTE

It was defined the "sad, harsh and severe house", "a house like me", by Curzio Malaparte, the great Italian writer who had it built on Punta Massullo at a point which would be somewhat of an understatement to define panoramic due to its indescribable beauty. The residence, built between 1938 and 1949 on a design by Adalberto Libera (the designer of the Congress Palace of Eur in Rome), stands out clearly, due to its original architecture, from the constructions typical of the island. Surrounded by a pinewood, it has a two-floor structure painted red, stretching out towards the

sea and interrupted only by the scenic steps that lead up to the solarium, a flat surface defined by a slight curve of white brick arranged in an arc, like a sail: some art critics have interpreted these features as an enchanting reference to the sacrificial altars of the ancient temples. The interiors, to which Curzio Malaparte made considerable changes with respect to Libera's design, are both simple and stylish at the same time. In the drawing-room, the writer had a large closed fireplace built, not set into a wall but into a large sheet of crystal from you can see the fire's flames, as if in a picture, with the Faraglioni and the Rock of Monacone in the background.

Curtius Malaparte's highly original villa at the tip of Punta Massullo

THE FARAGLIONI

The three famous gigantic rocks emerging from the water owe their characteristic form to the corrosion of the waters and action of the rain and wind. The first, known as "Faraglione Stella" or "Faraglioni di Terra" (111 m high), is joined to the island by a strip of land. On the second, the "Faraglione di Mezzo" (81 m high), there is the "subway", a remarkably large natural arch through which you can transit in a boat. The third Faraglione, known as the "Faraglione di Fuori" or "Faraglione Scopolo" (105 m high), is separated from the previous one by a narrow (8 m) stretch of sea and is the home of a special kind of lizard (blue lizard of the Faraglioni), the same colour as the sky and the sea.

Three magnificent pictures of the Faraglioni rock

ROCK OF MONACONE

Clearly visible from the belvedere of Punta Tragara, the rock, which is large enough to be classified a small island, owes its name to the monk seal, a species that is now extremely rare in the Mediterranean and extinct on Capri. Some believe that the name derives from the fact that, in ancient times, the monks of the Charterhouse of St. James came to live here like hermits for periods of spiritual retreat. At the top of the rock there are remains of a tank, believed to date back to Roman times and coated internally with lime, which gave rise to various interpretations about its functions during ancient times. In fact, the tank has been indicated as the tomb of Augustus' great architect, the Mauritanian Masgaba, or as the place where fish was dried or rain water was collected. It was apparently also used, during the period of French occupation, for the breeding of rabbits, where were then present in large numbers.

The great Rock of Monacone

GROTTA DI MATERMANIA

Situated about 180 m above sea level in the middle of a holm oak wood, this opening partially hidden by the thick vegetation can be reached by climbing up a steep flight of steps. The huge, semicircular cave (30 m long, 20 m wide and 10 m high) probably owes its name to the god of the land and fertility Cybele, in Latin "*Mater Magna*", to the worship of whom it was perhaps consecrated. It is certain that, during Augustus' and Tiberius' times, it was used as a large nymphaeum, as is witnessed by the Roman coating that can be seen on the walls. According to the research work carried out, archaeologists believe that inside the cave, in addition to some secondary rooms, the Romans had built a large hall with a reinforced vaulted ceiling to prevent the risk of collapse and a levelled floor to counteract the natural sloping of the ground. It was all coated with marble and mosaics (part of which were in all likelihood removed between the end of the 18th century and the 19th century, during Ferdinand IV's reign) and fitted out with seats and couches for those present to relax on.

The fascinating Grotta Matermania

THE NATURAL ARCH

The large natural rock arch, situated near Grotta di Matermania, where it dominates the creek of the same name, rises impressively to a height of about 200 m above sea level. Framed by a thick, wild vegetation, it forms one of the island's most enchanting pictures, which can be admired from the two panoramic terraces. The imposing rock was part of the vault of a gigantic cave, originally underground which geological movements, erosion and the action of the elements, over the millenniums, caused to collapse almost completely, leaving only this part standing. The central opening of the arch is the result of the collapse of another piece of rock, which spared the two lateral pillars.

A spectacular view of the "Natural Arch"

VILLA JOVIS

Built at the top of Mount Tiberius (334 m), the most impressive of the Roman villas on the island of Capri covers a surface area of over 6000 m². It was built by order of Emperor Tiberius, even though some slightly earlier finds brought to light during archaeological excavations in the area around the tanks suggested that Augustus had identified in that area an ideal place for building a residence. All in communication with one another by an intricate group of corridors, steps and passages, the various rooms of the villa, which probably occupied four floors on one side and two on the opposite side, were organized around an enormous rectangular area used for collecting rain water which, in turn, covered a tank with an extremely large capacity (in part built into the rock and in part made of brick) divided into several rooms designed for the same purpose. The imperial apartments, separated from the rest of the building and the magnificent loggia (over 90 m long) sheer above the sea and

Plan of Villa Jovis

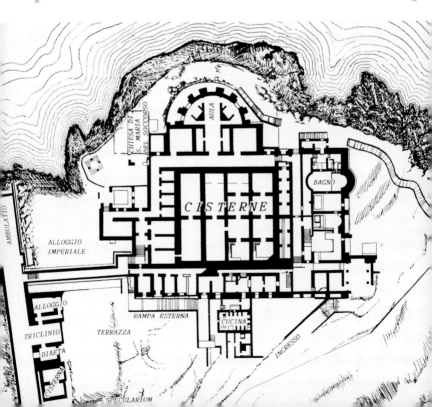

overlooking a splendid panorama, were situated on the North side, that is, in the area in which the view of the Gulf of Naples was more spectacular. On the opposite side, to the South, there was the spa area. On the East side, towards the Gulf of Salerno, there was the semi-circular hall of the guest quarters, with the various rooms for representation and the imperial chancellery, while on the West side were situated the kitchens and service rooms, such as warehouses and storehouses. To the South, at some distance from the ruins of the villa are those of the "Lighthouse Tower", along the outside of which runs a flight of steps that climbed up in a spiral around the walls. Despite its name, the construction was probably not used as a lighthouse for ships sailing off the island but, apparently, as a signalling tower used for communicating with other centres equipped with similar buildings. According to the tale, Tiberius even managed to communicate with Rome by means of a sort of "tam tam" based on smoke and fire signals, and to receive messages from the capital thanks to this tower, which thus enabled him to fulfil his imperial functions without leaving the island. The Roman historian Suetonius writes that, almost as a premonition, the tower collapsed as a result of an earthquake a few days before the emperor died. At a short

The ruins of the grand villa

distance from the lighthouse-tower you can see a precipice which, according to a tradition with no historical foundation was "Tiberius' leap", that is, the place off which the emperor made condemned men throw themselves. To the northeast, near the guest quarters, stands, on the villa ruins, the small church of St. Maria del Soccorso, which is even today a place of pilgrim for the island's fishermen who venerated the local Madonna. As early as the start of the 18th century, research work was carried out on the villa by order of the King of Naples, Charles III, aimed, as was often the case during this period, not at preserving but removing the marble, mosaics, wall decorations, furniture and valuables for transportation elsewhere or reuse as materials for other works. The same can be said, even more so, for the excavations carried out between the 18th and 19th centuries during Ferdinand IV's reign by Norbert Hadrawa who, here as elsewhere on the island, did not hesitate to strip the ruins of what he judged to be of value or worthy of interest. Further research work was carried out with a more scientific intention in 1827. Examples of the material removed during the course of these excavations which can be admired are a Roman floor rebuilt at the Royal Palace of Capodimonte, other marble floor decora-

Two views of the villa

tions in the church of St. Stephen, two marble puteals decorated in relief and one marble relief kept at the National Museum of Naples. The ruins, despite the fact that they were entrusted to the father of the church of St. Maria del Soccorso, were subsequently, in part, abandoned and overgrown by the vegetation and, in part, occupied by local shepherds and farmers with their activities. In 1932, a further campaign of excavations was finally organized, thanks to which the ruins were freed not only of their abusive occupants but also of the waste material that had accumulated there over the centuries and that, once removed, confirmed the "cultural sacking" of a large part of the embellishing works and even of part of the villa's structure. The archaeological area was inaugurated in 1937 on the two thousandth anniversary of Augustus' birth, as is indicated on a memorial tablet. Unfortunately, the ruins are currently in part covered by overgrown vegetation again and new work is necessary.

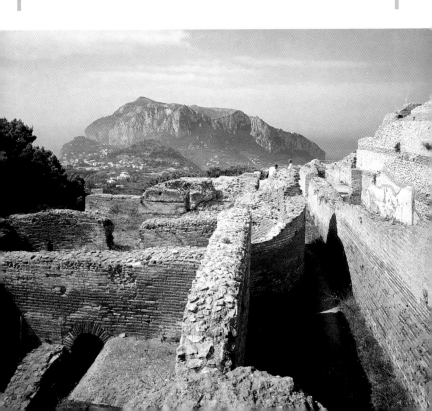

MARINA PICCOLA

The well-equipped tourist resort, which stretches along the southern coast of the island opposite Marina Grande, lies in an inlet on the slopes of Monte Solaro. From Capri you can reach it on foot starting from the Piazzetta first along via Roma and then via Marina Piccola. At a short distance from the cross-roads with the road that leads to Anacapri, in the vicinity of which stands the picturesque "Casa del Solitario", built into the rock of Monte Solaro open the caves including Grotta dell'Arco and Grotta delle Felci, in which prehistoric finds have been brought to light. There follows a section,

flanked by some beautiful private villas and gardens, which offers splendid views of the Faraglioni, Punta Tragara and the town of Marina Piccola. Going down towards the village, the road meets via Krupp and ends at the square in front of the small church of St. Andrew, built at the start of the century and restored at the end of the second world war to repair the serious damage caused by the explosion of a mine. Further on you come to the "Scoglio delle Sirene" (Mermaid's Rock), which has a small wharf and divides the inlet of Marina Piccola into two bays (Marina di Pennauto and Marina di Mulo) occupied by bathing establishments. If you take via Krupp, you come to the rocky beach of Torre Saracena, whose name calls to mind the raids by pirates who spread terror on the island during the 16th century.

A broad panorama of Marina Piccola

The bathing establishments at Marina Piccola

THE COAST SEEN FROM THE SEA

Starting from Marina Piccola and heading West you come to Grotta dell'Arco and Grotta delle Felci (in which Neolithic finds have been brought to light) and then, beyond Punta Mulo and Punta Ventroso, Grotta Verde (which takes its name from the emerald green colour of its water), the Grotta Rossa (named after the vegetation that grows on it) and Grotta Marmola. From Cala Marmolata open out the Grotta della Galleria, Grotta del Cannone (from the noise of the backwash), Grotta Brillante, Grotta dei Santi (with the characteristic rock formations that resemble figures praying) and Grotta Vela. You then continue on, beyond Punta del Tuono and Punta Carena, with its lighthouse, along the western, less rugged part of the coast (inland stand the Watch Tower and the towers of Materita and Damecuta) on which there are picturesque inlets (Limno, Tombosiello, di Mizzo and del Rio) interspersed with mini peninsulas and headlands. Having gone past Punta di Vetereto, you come to the small opening that leads into Grotta Azzurra, along the northern coast that rises up more and more steeply, and the ruins of Tiberius' Baths before reaching Marina Grande. Beyond the inlet are situated Grotta del Bue Marino and Grotta della Ricotta, followed by Punta del Cannone, beyond which the impressive rocky coast

The bathing establishments at Marina Piccola

The magical entrance to Grotta dei Santi

*Incredible rock forma-
tions:*

*Natural Arch
Grotta Verde
Grotta Meravigliosa
The tip of the headland
Grotta Bianca*

opens into Tiberius' Caves (in line with Tiberius' Leap), Grotta Bianca (with two stretches of fresh water inside, Grotta Meravigliosa (decorated with stalagmites) and Grotta dei Preti. Cala di Matermania, from which you can catch a glimpse of the Natural Arch, is followed by Punta Massullo (Casa Malaparte), the Rock of Monacone, Punta Tragara with the port of the same name and finally the Faraglioni. Before getting back to Marina Piccola, you pass the "Sailors' Hotel" with its blue-green water, the large Grotta della Certosa and, finally, Grotta dell'Arsenale, used as a nymphaeum in imperial times.

THE PHOENICIAN STEPS

Built halfway along the coast, the extremely steep steps climb almost vertically with a total of over five hundred steps along a winding path which connects Marina Grande to the town of Anacapri. Despite its name established by the tradition, the work was presumably started by the first Greek colonists to settle on Capri, who built some parts by laying blocks of stone and other parts by building them into the rock. Subsequently, as is witnessed by some remains dating back to imperial times, the steps were restored and modified by the Romans, who reduced their number, which was originally perhaps even more than eight hundred. It remained the only way of reaching Anacapri and the surrounding plateau from the sea until the mid 1870's, when the current road was built. The steps start near the Seaside Palace and end where there was once the Medieval arch with a drawbridge, which acted as a "border" between Capri and Anacapri, called the *"Porta della Diffidencia" or "Porta della Differencia"* (apparently to underline the never-appeased rivalry between Capri and Anacapri), near Villa St. Michael. About halfway up the steps, at an extremely panoramic point in which the steps cross the road, stands the small church of St. Anthony of Padua (the patron saint of Anacapri), characterized by an extremely simple and linear architectural style both inside and out. Also known as the Sailors' Chapel, it was probably built during the second half of the 17th century and extended with the addition of the sacresty and the bell tower and restored at the end of the 19th century.

The Phoenician Steps and Villa St. Michael

Surrounded by olive groves and vineyards, Anacapri, the second largest town on the island, is a tranquil tourist resort crossed by pleasant streets which reach the historical centre (Le Boffe, Caprile) and invite the visitor to discover its many beauties. The area was certainly inhabited in Roman times, as is witnessed by the many finds. During the Middle Ages, it was attacked several times by Turkish pirates but grew under the influence of the monks of the Charterhouse of St. James and Capri, from which it did not become independent until 1496. In the 19th century and the first half of the 20th century, it welcomed numerous artists and intellectuals (both Italian and foreign) attracted, like the Queen of Sweden by the poetry and beauty of the place. Associated with the name of the Swedish doctor and writer Axel Munthe, who had Villa St. Michael built there, the town possesses many churches (of particular interest are those of St. Michael, St. Sophia and St. Maria of Constantinople) which fit perfectly into a quiet setting of pretty, low white houses. Totally out of line with the dominant architectural style is the Red House, in the ancient town centre, an extremely elaborate tower built at the start of the century by order of an eccentric American colonel around the ruins of an ancient 16th century tower where the people of Anacapri were said to have locked up their womenfolk during the periods in which the men were forced to leave the village to work.

Panorama from Anacapri and a statue of Caesar Augustus in the foreground

From the thick vegetation emerges the whiteness of Villa St Michael

VILLA ST. MICHAEL

The villa was founded by Axel Munthe (Oskarshamn 1857 - Stockholm 1949), a Swedish doctor, philanthropist, writer and great lover of antiques. Enchanted by the beauty of the island of Capri on his first visit in 1876, he lived there for many years and around 1910 he was struck by a serious eye illness which forced him to retire to the Tower of Materita (which he owned together with the area on which the Castle of Barbarossa stands, Tower of Damecuta, the Watch-Tower and many areas of land), where the light was less intense than in Villa San Michele, to write his most famous literary work, "The History of St. Michael", published in London in 1929. Despite the fact that it is a literary and, in part, fictitious work, in which he inserted episodes or details about the villa that have little or nothing to do with its real history, the "History of St. Michael" is extremely useful for understanding Munthe's desire to create a residence in which he could surround himself with the

The main façade of Villa St. Michael

ancient objects that he loved so, recreating an area that resembled, as much as possible, the style and refinement of the ancient imperial villas on the island. In the immediate vicinity of Anacapri, Munthe purchased, from a carpenter by the name of Vincenzo, an area of land used for growing vine where the only buildings were a modest country house and the ruins of the chapel of St. Michael: subsequent research showed that there was, in ancient times, on the site, one of the twelve villas that Emperor Tiberius had built on Capri. In this area, starting from 1896, he then began to built the splendid residence that can still be admired today, remarkable as much for its wonderful position and highly original architecture as for the number of ancient finds kept there within, a large part of which does not, however, come from excavations carried out on the island of Capri. At the entrance to the villa, there is a simple wooden portal surrounded by a marble frieze with animal and vegetable motifs, which leads into the entrance hall, adorned with a remarkable Roman tombstone

A portrait of Axel Munthe

AXEL MUNTHE
1857 – 1949

and a mosaic floor with a design found at Pompei (Cave canem).

Another Pompeian mosaic floor ("Death and the Wine") can be admired in the dining-room, furnished in Renaissance style. At the centre of the building there is an open-air hall, based on a large-space design with the tanks for collecting rain water around which the imperial villas were organized. Right in the middle you can see a Roman puteal decorated with bas-reliefs; the walls are decorated with fragments of Roman terracotta and bronze heads. From this entrance hall climbs a flight of steps up to the loggia above, from which you enter the bedroom, which is also furnished in Italian Renaissance style and adorned with replicas of Pompeian bronzes and a

magnificent bas-relief of the Roman imperial period. Of particular interest is Axel Munthe's study where, in addition to the Roman copy of Aphrodite's head, a young man's head of the 4th century BC and the majestic mosaic floor which probably came from one of the imperial villas on the island, there is a Medusa's head: in the History of Saint Michael, Munthe writes that it was found on the bottom of Tiberius' Baths after a vision he had had in a dream but, in part due to its incredible resemblance with three famous sculptures of Medusa kept at the Vatican, it seems more plausible that it was purchased from an antique dealer. The Loggia of Sculptures is, however, the biggest attraction with its numerous statues, mostly late replicas of ancient

The fabulous villa gardens

originals, Roman fragments and other valuable works: the most outstanding is the marble bust (original) portraying Emperor Tiberius (according to some, however, it portrays his nephew Germanicus). From the loggia you move on to the pergola of the villa, overlooking the garden, with a lookout from which you get a wonderful view of the inlet of Marina Grande and the Gulf of Naples. At the bottom of the steps that lead up to the chapel, you can admire the remains of a wall in "opus reticulatum" belonging to the imperial villa which stood on the site in ancient times and other Roman ruins (the ruins of a cubicle and a floor from imperial times). The chapel, probably built shortly before the year 1000, was converted by Munthe into a library

View from the villa's panoramic lookout

and music hall: on the outside, the main wall is decorated with a splendid Roman tomb relief portraying a mother with her son, while inside there is a beautiful 14th century font. On the wall of the terrace that surrounds the chapel, Munthe set up an Egyptian sphinx which was, in all probability, but contrary to what the writer states in his literary work, a replica of an ancient sculpture. This part of the villa offers a splendid view of Castle of Barbarossa. Below the terrace you can see the terminal part of the Phoenician Steps which lead up from Marina Grande to Anacapri. Finally, from the chapel an avenue of cypresses (planted by the writer himself) leads back to the villa: at the end of the path you can admire Lucius Carcius' tomb, a Roman work dating

back to the 1st century BC. Shortly before his death, Munthe donated the villa to the Swedish State and it now houses the St. Michael Foundation, which is dedicated to humanist studies and research in the field of classical culture in general.

Statue of Artemis

Tiberius' bust

A glimpse of the Loggia with Hermes at rest in the foreground

A broad view of the Loggia

It was built between the 10th and 11th centuries by the inhabitants of the area around the town of Anacapri as a fortification to defend the town against the Saracens' raids which, accompanied by sacking, destruction and robbery, were extremely frequent even on the island of Capri. In memory of that terrible period there remains the name of the bulwark, Khair-ad-din, admiral of the Turkish fleet nicknamed Barbarossa who, in 1535 won over the resistance of the islanders and destroyed it almost completely. From the ruins, which rise up on a large sheer area (once covered by a beautiful pine forest which has been struck several times by violent fires) that dominate the sea, you can clearly identify the two towers belonging to the stone outer walls and, at the centre of the complex, a small chapel with an apse and barrel vault flanked by a bell tower. The castle (which houses an institute for the study

The sturdy outer walls of the Castle of Barbarossa

of ornithology) stands on an estate belonging to the Swedish Consulate, which organizes guided tours periodically both to the ruins and the surrounding area, of great naturalistic interest both for its fauna and flora.

A typical part of the castle

MONTE SOLARO AND THE CHAIR LIFT

Reaching an altitude of 589 m above sea level, the mountain, situated on the Western part of the island, is the highest peak on Capri. The summit, on which at the start of the century a large tourist complex (the "Sky's Song") was planned to be built but was never completed, can be reached from Anacapri by taking the chair lift (in about ten minutes) or on foot (about an hour and a half's walk) along a pleasant itinerary that winds along a path first through a wood of oaks and chestnuts and then is surrounded by a thick, low vegetation, offering marvellous panoramas. Together with the funicular railway which climbs up from Marina Grande to the town of Capri, the chair lift is certainly one of the most spectacular means of transport for admiring the island and its natural beauties. The bottom station is situated in the centre of Anacapri, at the end of Piazza della Vittoria, while the top station at an altitude of 586 m above sea level, is only three metres from the summit of Mount Solaro. Along the path, which runs along the western slope of the mountain, covered with woods, you can glance at the mountain, the plateau of Anacapri and the western coast of the island, offering one of the most varied and picturesque panoramas of the whole of Capri. The best view, magnificent and unforgettable, can be enjoyed from the summit of the

The unforgettable panorama to be enjoyed from Monte Solaro

mountain, where there are the ruins of a fortress built on the site of a pre-existent Medieval settlement by the English during the period of the war against the French (1806-08). From here you can admire not only the island, with the other lower peaks, white houses and villas scattered in the green countryside, the orchards, vineyards and olive groves, the coast modelled by the various headlands, the inlets and caves, the Faraglioni and rocks that emerge from the water, but also the Gulf of Sorrento and the Gulf of Naples, the peninsula of Sorrento, Ischia, Procida and even the Apennine peaks and, down below, the church of St. Maria Cetrella with its small hermitage. The hermitage, situated near the peak, can be reached in a few minutes by turning off (when you come to a small chapel dedicated to the Virgin Mary) the path that leads back to Anacapri. From the church, which dates back to the end of the 14th century and the early 15th century, standing on the edge of the rock face that overlooks Marina Piccola, there is a marvellous panorama of Capri and the surrounding area. St. Maria a Cetrella is a traditional place of pilgrimage for fishermen every year in October.

The chair lift that leads from Anacapri to Monte Solaro

74

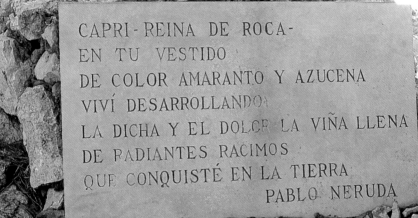

CAPRI · REINA DE ROCA ·
EN TU VESTIDO
DE COLOR AMARANTO Y AZUCENA
VIVÍ DESARROLLANDO
LA DICHA Y EL DOLOR LA VIÑA LLENA
DE RADIANTES RACIMOS
QUE CONQUISTÉ EN LA TIERRA
PABLO NERUDA

Picturesque spots on the island

THE CHURCH OF ST. SOPHIA

Easily identified by its characteristic dome, the church stands in Piazza Materita, once known as the "stone square". The building, which was built, according to the tradition, in 1510, was actually constructed towards the end of the 16th century on the site of a pre-existent church of Medieval origin dedicated to St. Charles. The date of 1510 probably refers (as indicated by an inscription on the façade) to its foundation, which took place the year which saw the abandonment of the 16th century parish church of S. Maria a Li Curti (today S. Maria of Constantinople, in the village of Carena, a short distance from the town of Anacapri). The church took on a certain historical importance around 1680, when the sailors of Anacapri, following the example set by the fishermen of Capri, founded the Pawnshop of S.Maria del Buoncamino at S. Sofia. This was one of the many institutions that flouri-

shed on the island starting 1680 (when the first pawnshops were opened on Capri), permitting the sailors, normally without great resources, to invest their earnings. The money was then used above all for the dowry of the fishermen's daughters when they got married or to help people who had found themselves out of work and were thus unable to maintain their families. The church (which was not consecrated until 1790) underwent several modifications during the course of the 17th and 18th centuries, which were carried out in various different periods and under the direction of various architects and engineers and thus resulted in the creation of a building in which differing styles are placed side by side in a disorderly or, at best, non-uniform fashion: the three-aisle interior, for example, has a barrel vault over the central aisle while the lateral aisles have domical vaults. The white façade, consisting of three parts and soberly decorated with stucco work, was built, like the bell tower, in the second half of the 18th century.

The picturesque façade of the church of St. Sophia

Detail of the church, the clock

THE CHURCH OF ST. MICHAEL ARCHANGEL

The temple, a baroque building constructed between the 17th and 18th centuries, was added, in the 18th century, to the existing Teresian convent of St. Michael, founded by Sister Serafina di Dio (1621-99). At the time Prudence of Nicole,Antonio di Pisa, was, together with St. Constant, the leading religious figure in the island's history. Though seemingly destined to live a life of wealth and luxury, the young woman chose to take her vows in the order of St. Teresa d'Avila.

During the course of her lifetime, she founded many monasteries including the monastery of St. Michael Archangel at Anacapri, built, according to the legend, in thanks to heaven for having crowned her wishes by protecting the city of Vienna from the Turkish raids. Completed in 1719, the church of St. Michael stood alongside the existing church of St. Nicholas of which traces remain and completed the monastic

The floor of the church of St. Michael, a precious work of art made of majolica.

nucleus planned by Sister Serafina. In 1808, with the advent of Napoleon's rule, the temple was closed: the Bourbons had it reopened but the church lived a troubled existence until almost the end of the century; it was even used as an ammunition depot and an orphanage before it was, in the end, sold to a Protestant German nobleman. The interior of the church, based on a central plan on which an octagonal dome was set, presents, in harmonious corners with apses, beautiful painted wooden altars, an impressive high altar made of marble decorated with hard stones and important canvases of the 17th and 18th centuries. The most remarkable work is the splendid majolica tile floor which stretches as far as the area delimited by the dome, laid in 1761 by a craftsman from Naples on commission by the Prince of St. Nicandro. It represents the expulsion of Adam and Eve from the Garden of Eden, inhabited by all kind of animals among which stands a unicorn at the centre of the composition.

The avenue and façade of the church of S. Maria at Constantinople

THE IMPERIAL VILLA OF DAMECUTA

Easily reached on foot from Anacapri (in about three quarters of an hour) along a pleasant itinerary through the vine and olive trees which offers splendid views of the island, the archaeological area of Villa of Damecuta is one of the most interesting in the whole of Capri. The results of the in-depth archaeological research work carried out between 1937 and 1948 did not succeed in determining whether the villa, which must have been one of the most magnificent of those built in the imperial period, was built during Augustus' or Tiberius' reign: the damage examined on the works brought

to light has enabled it to be established that the villa was abandoned after the eruption of Vesuvius in 79 AD (over forty years after the death of Augustus' successor), which had sprinkled this part of the island with ash and lava. This abandonment was probably for ever and, for the luxurious residence, marked the start of a dark period which was to bring it to almost total destruction: on the one hand, it was used in part as material for constructing fortifications and means of defence both against pirate raids in the Middle Ages and in the period of war between the English (allies of the Bourbons) and the French, and on the other, it was sacked and devastated on more than one occasion. Nevertheless, the state of destruction and scarcity of

The gigantic tower of Damecuta

finds must not be attributed exclusively to the military troops that settled among the ruins of the villa or the islanders who abusively occupied the areas with all sorts of activities over the centuries but also, in all likelihood, as at Villa Jovis, to "cultural sacking" perpetrated above all between the 18th and 19th centuries by self-styled archaeologists (above all, the Austrian art merchant Norbert Hadraw), and antique lovers. For a combination of all these factors, there are very few remains, not even enough to attempt to reconstruct what the original structure of the building was like. It can only therefore be supposed that Villa Damecuta, like all the other imperial residences on the island, was extremely large and divided into many rooms linked to one another and embellished with stylish decorative works (the remains of columns, marble statues and sections of wall constructed in *opus reticulatum* have been found, but there must also have been mosaic floors, wall paintings and other ornaments) and surrounded by gardens. Here too, as in Villa Jovis, was found a gigantic tank for collecting rain water, necessary above all for the shortage of rain in the area. The only clearly identifiable part of the residence is a long loggia with a portico overlooking the sea

The ruins of the imperial loggia of the Villa of Damecuta

that runs along the promontory; the western side ends with a semicircular belvedere (around which there was a series of rooms) from which you get a spectacular panorama. At the eastern end, archaeologists have brought to light the remains of a small drawing room and another much smaller belvedere. Nearby, on the perimeter of the villa, there is a watch tower built in the 12th century; it was purchased by Axel Munthe, who donated it to the Italian State together with the entire villa area, which also belonged to him.

The "opus reticulatum" ruins of the Villa of Damecuta

BLUE CAVE

It is certainly the most famous place on the island of Capri, the most spectacular and without doubt, at least during the tourist season, one of the most crowded. Its name and beauty are due to the intense blue colour of the crystal-clear water in this cave formed over the millenniums by the erosive action of the sea. The cave consists of several enclosures: the largest of these, known as the "Duomo Azzurro" (Blue Cathedral), which is accessed through a natural opening artificially widened in Roman times and around 1830, covers a surface area of about 70 m in length, 25 in width and

20-22 in depth: the height of the internal vault ranges from 7 to 14 m. From this main cavity lead many corridors and passages to other underground ravines. The fact that the water is blue (Sèvres blue, as the colour is known, due to its resemblance to the famous French pottery) depends on physical factors in that it only filters the blue component of light from the outside which enters the cave through an underwater opening situated directly below the entrance. Due to the same physical effect, any object immersed in the water (which only becomes blue when the sea is slightly rough) turns a silver colour. Research and studies conducted over the years have suggested that Grotta Azzurra was a Roman nymphaeum (that is, a place consecra-

The charm and enchantment of the extraordinary stretch of sea at the entrance to Grotta Azzurra

ted to the worship of nymphs), belonging perhaps to the Augustan villa called Gradola (from which the cave borrowed its name until the 1828 explorations, when it was renamed Grotta Azzurra), built on the embankment overlying the cave: evidence backing up this theory includes the numerous statues found in cave's water during the Sixties and more recently, probably fixed to the walls of the cave originally, and the internal landing-place which can be seen on the right-hand side of the entrance, a sort of artificial platform. In 1826, an Austrian painter, August Kopfish, explored the cave, accompanied by a friend and two islanders, gave it the name Grotta Azzurra and, from that moment on, was recognized as its modern-day discove-

The lights, colours and magic of the fascinating Grotta Azzurra

rer. In reality, the place was known, by the name of Grotta di Gradola, at least as early as the 17th century. It became famous throughout Europe starting from the first half of the 19th century as a result of the romantic and enchanting descriptions given by many artists (writers, painters and musicians) who came to visit it.

Situated at a height of 292 m above sea level, it is one of the most panoramic points in the whole of Capri. Starting from Anacapri, it can be reached from the small Piazza di Caprile along the pleasant Migliara road, which climbs gradually, offering splendid views of Anacapri and the open sea as far as the island of Ischia. Once the road, which winds its way along the path of a more ancient road, was completely immersed in the countryside and surrounded by vineyards, orchards and woods, while today, particularly in the initial part, you come across a large number of villas

and houses. The belvedere opens at the start of the small peninsula that juts out to sea with Punta Carena, dominated by the lighthouse tower. The panorama over the area below and the sea is marvellous, and you get an even more breathtaking view from the left-hand side of the belvedere, towards Punta del Tuono: the view here starts from the beautiful Cala Marmolata and goes beyond Marina Piccola to Punta Tragara and the Faraglioni, sweeping across the entire southern shore of the island, with the white, sheer rock faces, sprayed with the green colour of the vegetation, the inlets and the ravines that decorate the coast like precious inlays and the unforgettable blue colour of the sea that laps the entire rugged shoreline.

The ancient fortifications of the Belvedere of Migliara

THE WATCH TOWER

The circular tower was built by order of the Spanish viceroys as a means of defence against attacks from the nearby Punta Carena. It stands at a height of about 300 metres above sea level at an extremely attractive point of the coast on the cliffs that dominate the Cala del Tombosiello and Cala del Limmo below, from which you get a wonderful panorama. After a period of abandonment, it was restored and converted into a private residence. From the Watch Tower, you can reach both Punta Carena and the Belvedere of Migliara by following a short and picturesque itinerary.

Watchtower over the majestic cliffs that dominate the sea

THE TOWER OF MATERITE

Presumably built in the 16th century by the Carthusians monks from the monastery of St. James in Capri to defend themselves against pirate raids, the tower was abandoned after the monks were expelled following the suppression (1808) of the Charterhouse of St. James ordered by Napoleon's government and remained deserted until the start of the present century. In 1900 it was purchased by Axel Munthe, who had it restored and, having been struck by a serious eye illness which prevented him from being able to bear bright light, he found relief residing there from 1910 to 1943; it was here that in 1929-29, he wrote his famous work *"The History of St. Michael"*.

PUNTA CARENA

It is reached from Anacapri along a road bordered in its initial section by villas and characteristic Capri houses and, further on, immersed in a wilder panorama dominated by the colour of the rock and low vegetation typical of the island. The headland, which forms the tip of the small peninsula of Migliara, delimiting a sort of natural border between the western coast and the southern coast of Capri, projects a short distance from the belvedere of Migliara out to the open sea with its impressive cliffs that drop vertically forming huge rock steps and plunge into the water below. The flat end of the headland is dominated by the impressive lighthouse. Resting on a square white building, the white and red tower with an octagonal plan, still in operation today, was built at an extremely panoramic and clearly visible point, even from the open sea, in 1866. Over the years, Punta Carena, which represents an excellent point of observation over the surrounding area, was also employed for military purposes, as is witnessed by the constructions in the surrounding area: a fortress dating back to the early years of the 19th century, which was used by the French and English troops during the period of occupation, and a watchtower where the sentinels could shelter, built during the second world war. Moving on further west, you come to the bathing area known by the name "Bagni del Faro" (Lighthouse Baths), from which you can admire, towards the inland area, the Watch Tower, which rises up in a strategic position, dominating the Cala del Tombosiello.

The wild precipice of Punta Carena

USEFUL INFORMATION

SERVICES OF PUBLIC INTEREST.

LOCAL TOURIST BOARD, Tourist Information Offices, Capri, tel. 837.0686; Marina Grande, tel. 837.1524 - POLICE: tel. 113 - STATE POLICE STATION; Via Roma, tel. 837.7245-837.7246 - MILITARY POLICE STATION: Capri, Via Prov. M. Grande, tel. 837.0000; Anacapri - Via G.Orlandi, tel. 837.1011 - FIRST AID STATION (NIGHT AND HOLIDAY SERVICE): tel 837.5019 - HARBOUR OFFICE: Local Shipping Office: Marina Grande, tel. 837.0226 - CAPRI TOWN COUNCIL: Piazza Umberto I, tel. 837.0054-837.0688 - ANACAPRI TOWN COUNCIL: Via Caprile, tel. 837.1012-837.1703 - POST OFFICES: Capri, Via Roma, tel. 837.7240; Marina Grande, Via Provinciale M.Grande, tel. 837.7229; Anacapri, viale T.De Tommaso, tel 837.1015 - TRAFFIC WARDENS: Capri, Piazza Umberto I, tel 837.0054-837.0688; Anacapri, Via Caprile, tel. 837.2423 - PUBLIC TELEPHONES: Capri, Piazza Umberto I, tel. 837.5550; Anacapri, Piazza Vittoria, tel 837.3377 - HOSPITAL: Capilupi, Via Provinciale, Anacapri, tel 837.0014-837.8762: CHEMIST'S: Capri, Farmacia Internazionale, via Roma, tel 837.0485; Farmacia Quisisana, Via V.Emanuele I, tel 837.0185; Anacapri, Farmacia Barile, Piazza Vittoria, tel 837.1460 - CHURCHES: Catholic in Capri and Anacapri, Evangelical (German) at Capri, Via Tragara.

VARIOUS PUBLIC SERVICES

THE MARINA GRANDE-CAPRI FUNICULAR RAILWAY: The funicular runs every 15' from 6.30 a.m. to 10 p.m. After this time, there is a bus service along the same route with a bus every 30'. TOURIST TRIPS TO THE ISLAND: Consorzio Noleggiatori Capresi (Hirers' Association of Capri) tel. 837.1544-837.2422. BUS: Public Service - Capri - Anacapri and back; Capri - Marina Piccola and back; Capri - Damecuta and back; Marina Grande-Anacapri and back; Marina Piccola-Anacapri and back - SIPIC, tel 837.0420. Public Service: Anacapri-Grotta Azzurra and back; Anacapri-Faro and back STAIANO AUTOTRASPORTI, tel. 837.1544. TAXI: Capri, tel. 837.0543; Anacapri, tel. 837.1175 CHAIR LIFT OF MONTE SOLARO: Anacapri, tel. 837.1428. From Anacapri (296 m a.s.l.) to Monte Solaro (586 m a.s.l.). The trip takes 12 minutes. Open:non-stop from 9 a.m. till sunset. MOTORBOATS: Marina Grande, Gruppo Motoscafisti, tel. 837.5646: Marina Grande-Grotta Azzurra and back; trip round the island (minimum 15 passengers).

USEFUL ADDRESSES

SOCIETA' DI NAVIGAZIONE DEL GOLFO (GULF SHIPPING COMPANY): Aliscafi Alilauro, tel. 837.7577, Aliscafi Medmar, tel. 837.7577, Aliscafi SNAV, tel 837.7577 (Hydrofoils), Caremar (Hydrofoils and Steamboats), tel. 837.0700, Giuffrh & Lauro tel. 837.6171, Free Navigation in the Gulf and Jet line, tel. 837.0819

TRAVEL OFFICES: Capri: Grotta Azzurra - Via Roma, tel 837.0466/837.0702; Tiberio Viaggi e Turismo, Via Camerelle 6, tel 837.6376/837.6371, fax 837.8933.

Marina Grande: Grotta Azzurra - Largo Fontana, tel.
837.0410/837.7528, fax 837.7528.
Anacapri: Pansa Travel, Via G.Orlandi 21/b, tel. 837.2230

EXCHANGE OFFICES: Capri, Cambio - Via Roma 33 (9 a.m. - 7 p.m.), tel. 837.0785; La Piazzetta - Piazza Umberto I (9 a.m. - 8 p.m.), tel 837.0557 Post office, Via Roma. Marina Grande: La Piazzetta, Via C.Colombo 63 (9 a.m. 6 p.m.), tel. 837.8866. Anacapri: La Piazzetta 2, Piazza Vittoria, 2 bis, tel. 837.3146.

ANCIENT RUINS, MUSEUMS, LIBRARIES, ETC.

TIBERIUS' PALACE: Tiberius' imperial villa. The largest and most luxurious of Tiberius' residences, built in the 1st century after Christ - Open: weekdays and holidays from 9 a.m. till one hour before sunset.
IMPERIAL VILLA OF DAMECUTA: Open from 9 a.m. till 5 p.m.. One of the 12 villas that Tiberius had built on Capri during the 1st century A.D.. Its ruins, which were brought to the light during excavations between 1937 and 1948, can clearly be seen. At the East end of the Loggia, a cylindrical tower (the tower of Damecuta) was built in the Middle Ages (12th century) to defend it from the pirate raids typical of the period.
AXEL MUNTHE'S VILLA OF ST. MICHAEL: Built by the Swedish writer and doctor Axel Munthe on the ruins of an ancient Roman residence, it is an impressive construction with great freedom of style. It contains archaeological finds from the Roman period found on Capri. Open: January-February: 10.30 a.m. - 3.30 p.m., March: 9.30 a.m. - 4.30 p.m., April: 9.30 a.m. - 5 p.m., May-September: 9 a.m. - 6 p.m., October: 9.30 a.m. - 5 p.m., November-December: 10.30 a.m. - 3.30 p.m..
CHURCH OF ST. MICHAEL. The floor of this church, a magnificent majolica carpet, depicts Adam and Eve in the Garden of Eden. The floor was painted during the second half of the 17th century by Leonardo Chiaiese, a famous majolica maker from Abruzzo. Open: 9 a.m. - 2 p.m.. GROTTA AZZURRA: Visits every day from 9 a.m. to one hour before sunset. Motorboat from Marina Grande. The Grotta Azzurra can also be reached by land, starting from Anacapri and following the road that starts at the windmill and winds its way to the Grotta.
CHARTERHOUSE OF ST. JAMES: Founded by Giacomo Arcucci from Capri, the secretary of Joan I, the Queen of Naples, in the 14th century. The most ancient part is constituted by the church and 14th century cloisters. It contains a collection of paintings from the 17th to 19th centuries including the painter KURT W. DIEFENHACH's collection. There is a section where cyclic ancient and modern art exhibitions are held. There are also halls for congresses and cultural meetings. Open every day from 9 a.m. to 2 p.m.. Closed on Mondays.
"IGNAZIO CERIO" CENTRE: Non-profit corporation. Library with a collection of books and publications about Capri. A museum with a collection of fossils from the Palaeolithic. Rooms for conferences and concerts. Cultural and various other events. Open: 10 a.m. - 12 p.m. Mondays to Fridays.
"IGNAZIO CERIO" CENTRE LIBRARY: Piazzetta I, Cerio 5, tel. 837.0858. Open: Tuesdays, Thursdays and Saturdays from 5-8 p.m.; Wednesdays and Fridays from 10 a.m. to 1 p.m..

INDEX

© COPYRIGHT - KINA ITALIA S.p.A. - Milan
Page lay-out and printers - KINA ITALIA S.p.A. - Milano
Text: Claudia Converso
Translations: ATD Milano
All rights to photographs and text reserved

L. 7.000

Chicken Soup for the Soul®
Cartoons for Teachers

CHICKEN SOUP
FOR THE SOUL®
CARTOONS FOR TEACHERS

Jack Canfield
Mark Victor Hansen
John McPherson,
Creator of *Close to Home*

Health Communications, Inc.
Deerfield Beach, Florida

www.bcibooks.com
www.chickensoup.com

CLOSE TO HOME ©2003 *John McPherson. Reprinted with permission of Universal Press Syndicate.* www.ucomics.com.

For information on reprinting any cartoons in this book, please go to *www.amureprints.com.*

Library of Congress Cataloging-in-Publication Data

McPherson, John, date.
    Chicken soup for the soul : cartoons for teachers / [compiled by] Jack Canfield,
  Mark Victor Hansen ; [cartoons by] John McPherson.
      p.   cm.
    ISBN-13: 978-0-7573-0149-0 (TP)
    ISBN-10: 0-7573-0149-5 (TP)
    1. Teaching—Caricatures and cartoons. 2. Teachers—Caricatures and cartoons.
  3. American wit and humor, Pictorial. I. Canfield, Jack, date. II. Hansen,
  Mark Victor. III. Title.

NC1429.M275A4 2004
741.5'973—dc22

                                                  2003060071

Publisher: Health Communications, Inc.
           3201 S.W. 15th Street
           Deerfield Beach, Florida 33442-8190

Cover design by Larissa Hise Henoch
Inside formatting by Dawn Von Strolley Grove

Other books by John McPherson

Chicken Soup for the Soul® Cartoons for Moms
Close to Home
Dangerously Close to Home
One Step Closer to Home
The Silence of the Lamberts
Close to Home Revisited
Home: The Final Frontier
Close to Home Unplugged
Striking Close to Home
The Close to Home Survival Guide
The Get Well Book
High School Isn't Pretty
Close to Home Uncut
The Scourge of Vinyl Car Seats
Close to Home Exposed
The Honeymoon Is Over

Acknowledgments

We wish to express our heartfelt gratitude to the following people who helped make this book possible:

Our publisher, Peter Vegso, for his vision and commitment to bringing *Chicken Soup for the Soul* to the world.

Patty Aubery and Russ Kamalski, for being there on every step of the journey with love, laughter and endless creativity.

Nancy Autio, Barbara LoMonaco, Heather McNamara and D'ette Corona for spearheading this project throughout the various phases of its completion. Thank you for helping with the final selection of cartoons.

Maria Nickless and Stephanie Thatcher, for their enthusiastic marketing and public relations support and brilliant sense of direction.

Patty Hansen, for her thorough and competent handling of the legal and licensing aspects of the *Chicken Soup for the Soul* books. You are magnificent at the challenge!

Laurie Hartman, for being a precious guardian of the *Chicken Soup* brand.

Jack and Mark's wonderful staff, who support their businesses with skill and love. Thanks to Mike Foster, Teresa Esparza, Leslie Riskin, Veronica Romero, Robin Yerian, Jesse Ianniello, Jody Emme, Debbie Lefever, Michelle Adams, Dee Dee Romanello, Shanna Vieyra, Lisa Williams, Gina Romanello, Brittany Shaw, Dena Jacobson, Tanya Jones, Mary McKay and David Coleman.

Bret Witter, Lisa Drucker, Allison Janse, Susan Heim and Genene Hirschhorn, our editors at Health Communications, Inc., for their devotion to excellence.

Terry Burke and the marketing and public-relations departments at Health Communications, Inc., for doing such an incredible job supporting our books.

The art department at Health Communications, Inc., for their talent, creativity and unrelenting patience in producing book covers and inside designs that capture the essence of *Chicken Soup*: Larissa Hise Henoch, Lawna Patterson Oldfield, Andrea Perrine Brower, Anthony Clausi and Dawn Von Strolley Grove.

Thank you to all of the *Chicken Soup for the Soul* coauthors, who make it so much of a joy to be part of this *Chicken Soup* family.

To Greg Melvin, Lee Salem, Denise Clark, Sadie Webb and the other great folks at Universal Press Syndicate for their ongoing support of John and his work.

Special thanks to John Vivona and the Universal Press sales force for their hard work on John's behalf. You guys are the best.

Lastly, thanks to Chris Millis, John's right-hand man.

We are truly grateful and love you all!

Introduction

Your days are spent dodging spitballs, fielding homework excuses and battling the class clown for attention. Evenings find you grading homework and getting the sound of ringing bells out of your head. And you wouldn't have it any other way.

Chances are, you wanted to be a teacher from a very young age. Chances are, another teacher, just like you, ignited that spark in you to become an educator. He or she made it a joy to learn, and encouraged your talents and skills. So the tradition continues, the torch is passed, and it is your turn now. It is up to you to inspire, entertain and enlighten a whole new generation of children. Our hats are off to you. You are heroes to your students.

Within this collection of cartoons, we hope that you will also see yourself as you really are: an entertainer, a cheerleader, a comedian, a guardian and a counselor. May these cartoons make you remember what made you want to be a teacher in the first place. Most importantly, may these cartoons provide you with much-needed comic relief after a long day in the classroom.

And if you're a student, we hope this book gives you a new perspective on those sometimes wonderful, sometimes horrible thirty hours a week you spend in class. Teachers aren't all out to get you— even the ones that, as you'll learn in this book, really do have extrasensory powers, the latest in child-zapping devices and a serious ax to grind!

So step away from that chalkboard, teachers around the world. Separate yourself from your red pen, put your feet up on your desk and give yourself a time out. You deserve it more than anyone.

Teaching is the choicest of professions because everybody who is anybody was taught how to be somebody by a teacher.

Source Unknown

Charlene soon began to realize that being the
teacher's pet wasn't all it was cracked up to be.

Eager to earn the $200 that had been raised
by his co-workers, Stan attempts to eat every
speck of crud from inside of the faculty microwave.

Many people would sooner die than think. In fact they do.

Bertrand Russell, English philosopher and social reformer

Unfortunately, Brad had neglected to stretch his brain before taking the big algebra midterm.

Wanting to save his parents thousands in
orthodontic costs, Lyle makes braces
for himself in metal shop.

"Well, when you get your grades up to a
B average, THEN you can choose
your own wallpaper."

Hoping to instill more pride in academics,
Oakfield High devised report card T-shirts.

Whiff-A-Leftover is becoming a popular game
in many company lunchrooms.

Mrs. Petibone uncovers an elaborate
cheating operation.

As he settled into the chair in the principal's office, Brian quickly noticed the desperate scratch marks made by previous visitors.

Unable to bear the humiliation of having her geeky dad drop her off at school, Amanda insisted that he dress as a rock star.

Nobody at Ben Franklin Senior High was
too psyched about the school's new dress code.

*Good teaching is one-fourth preparation
and three-fourths theater.*

Gail Godwin

"They always were a tight little clique."

Stricken by a sudden case of laryngitis,
Mrs. Gurtley switches to autoteacher.

Wes Lunker uses a visual aid to enhance
his report on the solar system.

Woodshop student Danny Curdleman
demonstrates his combination
bird feeder/napkin holder.

Replacement teacher Ellen Twitchell
has a sudden sense of foreboding.

*Education is not the filling of a pail,
but the lighting of a fire.*

William Butler Yeats

The Fegley High Drama Club presents
its adaptation of "Jaws."

Equipped with a series of tiny microphones under her fingernails and a 200-watt amplifier, Mrs. Raffner relished the moment she spotted a student dozing off.

"Thank you Barbara. Next, David Lombardo
will give his presentation on the
ancient city of Pompeii."

*The job of an educator is to teach students
to see the vitality in themselves.*

Joseph Campbell

"Did I mention the comment I made at
last night's school board meeting?"

Thoroughly burned-out by shuttling her kids
to and from school activities, Shelley makes
a drastic move.

The year the SAT creators decided
to mess with students' minds.

Before introducing herself to a class,
substitute teacher Rosetta Harg liked
to perform a brief karate demonstration.

"You heard me, Mendrick!
No hands or feet allowed!"

"His parents want to make sure
they don't miss seeing him take his first steps."

Tired of being picked last in gym class,
Kyle and Louis team up.

Having discovered a faint pulse in his lab frog,
Doug quickly began CPR.

Much have I learned from my teachers,
more from my colleagues, but most from my students.

Talmud

Tensions during final exams rose even higher
when it was learned that talent scouts
from "Jeopardy!" would be watching.

If you can read this, thank a teacher.

Bumper Sticker

"This isn't what I had in mind
when I signed up for shop class."

Rather than subject students, families and faculty to another monotonous graduation ceremony, the administration at Permfeld High asked students to log onto its Web site and print out their diplomas.

Knowing that he could make 50 cents a tooth
from the "Tooth Fairy," Alan makes
a killing at school.

Ted makes a failed attempt to bring back
the stovepipe hat.

With the meeting dragging on interminably,
Darrel hit the secret burst-water-pipe button.

Eleventh-grade algebra teacher Doris Snagleman
devises a creative way to save for
her new BMW convertible.

With the help of Hank Williams, Mrs. Slatchner
sends a subtle message to her students
during midterms.

Mr. Zorski's new anti-drowsiness
detection system worked like a charm.

The mediocre teacher tells.
The good teacher explains.
The superior teacher demonstrates.
The great teacher inspires.

William Arthur Ward

When teachers telecommute.

"You hop in there, she'll untie you, and then you tell her you were kidnapped over the weekend and couldn't get the term paper done."

Stu and Reggie orchestrate
an elaborate cheating scam.

In an attempt to toughen its graduation standards,
Wilmot High School now required students to answer
one last question before receiving their diploma.

Freshman Romney Yorp devised a foolproof way
to keep himself from getting lost.

Tina reacts to Principal Harstein's comment
that her third-grader, Jenny, has
difficulty handling criticism.

As the band continued to play, an angry mob
searched for members of the prom committee.

Every September, school buses everywhere
incur millions of dollars of damage by
souvenir-scavenging parents of kindergarteners.

With book loads on the rise, many students
are opting for the new Helium Backpacks.

Hoping to impress the chicks, Daryl had his
SAT scores tattooed on his right arm.

If you are planning for a year, sow rice;
if you are planning for a decade, plant trees;
if you are planning for a lifetime, educate people.

Chinese proverb

After being struck in the neck by a spitball, junior
high teacher and former Hollywood stuntman
Ed Delaney pulls one over on his students.

It didn't take much to upset Mrs. Stegler.

How teachers decide which students
to call on in class.

Mrs. Lasky hoped that oral midterms in
Spanish 201 would give students a
unique cultural experience.

Crystal lucks into being assigned
the legendary locker number 379.

How teachers prepare for an
upcoming school vacation.

"This dark area right here is my dog's stomach.
Now if you look closely, you can just make out
the title and first line of my term paper. . . ."

"...and when you come back and show me that
your parents have signed your report cards,
THEN the cuffs can come off."

*The object of teaching a child
is to enable him to get along without his teacher.*

Elbert Hubbard

Deep down inside, Coach Knott had always
wanted to be a math teacher.

"I must warn you, Ms. Maxwell,
I can read lips backward!"

The school's new hall passes proved to be
extremely effective in discouraging
frivolous trips to the rest room.

Thanks to the same technology that bank
drive-through windows rely on, frenzied parents
no longer need to worry about their kids missing the school bus.

Fortunately, Mrs. Gratchman's Thumbtack
Detection System spared her a trip
to the school nurse.

Wally fails the parallel parking portion of his exam.

Mr. Sinclair's woodshop class was slowly
starting to catch on to his weekly "field trip" scam.

The invention of the fax machine has taken
some of the charm out of passing notes in class.

A revolutionary breakthrough in driver
education technology: Nerf cars.

A diabolical new testing technique: math essay questions.

"OK, today we test your reflexes."

Long before he became famous as the host of "Jeopardy," Alex Trebek was a high school science teacher.

To prevent them from being taken advantage of
by unruly students, substitute teachers at Glencrest Junior High
underwent an extensive make-up session each morning.

More and more students are turning to
private coaching firms to help them
score higher on the SAT.

Unable to find a Hi-Liter, Wayne Merlman
used a black Magic Marker to cross out
all the stuff he didn't want to read again.

Mike would know better than to raise his hand
the next time Mr. Ferncod asked for a
volunteer to erase the blackboard.

Daryl's new hand enhancer dramatically improved his chances of being called on in class.

As school officials searched for the perpetrators,
an EMT wheeled away the dazed but unharmed victims
of The Great Locker Stuffing Incident of 2002.

Every person is gifted in some area.
We just have to find out what.

Evelyn Blose Holman

After acing five consecutive calculus tests,
Duane was able to land a lucrative endorsement deal.

"My dog ate my homework."

Just as the upperclassmen were about to
close the door, Lenny activated his
inflatable Anti-Locker-Stuffing Suit.™

Sensitive to the feelings of those kids
who routinely got picked last for teams, gym coach
Ray Mulnak devised a more humane player selection method.

Winston Central School District
finds a solution to overcrowded classrooms.

How most college students decide on a major.

Don't tell them how to do it, show them how to do it
and don't say a word. If you tell them,
they'll watch your lips move.
If you show them, they'll want to do it themselves.

Maria Montessori

To eliminate the buildup of noxious leftovers,
the faculty refrigerator was equipped
with an automatic purge valve.

"I think you've made your point!"

Striving to avoid a tuition hike, Dawson University
looked for other ways to generate revenue.

*You can lead a boy to college,
but you cannot make him think.*

Elbert Hubbard

How most high school students choose a college.

Not wanting to look like a loser for eating alone
in the cafeteria, Lyle brought along
his new Inflatable Lunch Pal.™

To help better prepare its students for
the real world, Raston University simulates
actual office conditions during final exams.

"Whoa! Not so fast, hotshot! The librarian says
you're not graduating until you return the copy of
Green Eggs and Ham you've had out since March of 1986!"

When high school students dream.

Hoping to catch some discreet Z's
during the film in biology, Brian brings
his head-prop and plastic eyeballs.

The Creedmont High class of 2000
dazzles the commencement audience with
a display of synchronized graduation cap tossing.

In an effort to emphasize both physical fitness
and academics, officials at
Westbury High devised aerobic algebra.

Suspecting that just such a word problem
might be on the algebra midterm, Gary came prepared.

Metal-shop teacher Hank Borgner
prided himself on his back-to-basics curriculum.

With homework assignments steadily on the rise, many students have opted for a more substantial way to carry their books.

"I know that many of you are squeamish about
dissecting a frog, so as an incentive, three of the frogs
have been implanted with concert tickets to Smashing Pumpkins."

How to tell when it's time to wash your gym socks.

Thanks to her new Virtual Reality Pod,
Mrs. Hacker was able to have parents
experience a school day with their child.

"My typewriter broke, so I had to do
my term paper on the Etch A Sketch."

Mike pulls the old "fake splinter" gag in wood shop.

"So den, weez tie on t'ree cinderblocks, and . . .
BADA-BING! . . . Down to da bottom he goes!
And dat was da last time anybody saw Bennie Da Mole!"

Mrs. Mutner liked to go over
a few of her rules on the first day of school.

"Cosgrove, get back here!"

It was only July, but already the dreaded
signs began to appear.

Knowing that she had already blown
her driver's test with her lousy parallel parking,
Karen decided to have a little fun with the examiner.

Knowing that one substitute alone could not
endure a full day in Mrs. Turbock's infamous fifth-grade
class, Principal Eckley made sure to line up eight subs.

The pressure of the SAT finally pushes
Brian Folbert over the edge.

Thanks to his new porcupine body suit,
Lenny was no longer easy prey for bullies.

"If anyone tries to look at someone else's
answers and turns his or her head
a mere three inches—TIMBER!"

A teacher was trying to impress her first-grade pupils
that good penmanship was important.
"Remember," she said, "if you don't learn to sign your name,
you'll have to pay cash for everything when you grow up."

Bits & Pieces

"My dog ate it."

"I thought the tassel looked a little bland
so I had it permed."

Copy from one, it's plagiarism; copy from two, it's research.

Wilson Mizner (1876–1933)

Teacher conference days: the *real* story.

High school principal Walt Mustin liked to
incorporate his love of TV game shows
into his work.

Jason proves that he wasn't lying
about the fate of his homework.

Thanks to his new Math Patch,™ Brad was able
to ace the algebra midterm in less than 12 minutes.

"Your diploma's not going to be ready for another two weeks, plus it turns out your tuition is going to be about $1,200 more than we originally estimated."

"Thank you, Erik, for that vivid
presentation on meteor showers."

A failed experiment in high school sports:
cross-country cheerleaders.

*My heart is singing for joy this morning.
A miracle has happened! The light of understanding
has shown upon my little pupil's mind,
and behold, all things are changed.*

Anne Sullivan

"Good morning, and welcome to
The Wonders of Physics."

*If someone is going down the wrong road,
he doesn't need motivation to speed him up.
What he needs is education to turn him around.*

Jim Rohn

"In all fairness, you never covered
'Bridge out' signs in class."

Every year during finals, Mr. Garmon flushes out
several cheaters with the same bluff.

With the school nurse out of the building,
Todd's broken arm was cared for
by the third period health class.

With final exams in full swing, the administration
brought out the cheat-sheet-sniffing dogs.

"Fred just retired after 32 years
as a driver's ed. teacher."

"Before we begin today's dissection lab,
I'd like you each to select your lab specimen
and take it back to your lab table."

Tired of their kids missing the bus each morning,
the Figbys ingeniously arranged to have
bus driver Vern Hickle move in with them.

To save time when signing yearbooks,
the more popular students at
Wagmont High relied on rubber stamps.

"I'm sure you'll find today's dissection
both challenging and enlightening."

Don's ant-farm shirt easily took
first place at the science fair.

Let's face it. Everybody does this when
they're assigned a 2,000-word term paper.

Students weren't too fond of the
new enlarged report cards.

Just when failing the geography midterm
seemed certain, Mike made an astonishing discovery.

Teachers open the door, but you must enter by yourself.

Chinese proverb

"Hey, Mike, I think you forgot your lunch again."

Algebra teacher Bert Fegman
was a master of reverse psychology.

Fortunately, Brian had the foresight to wear a
locker-stuffing escape kit at all times.

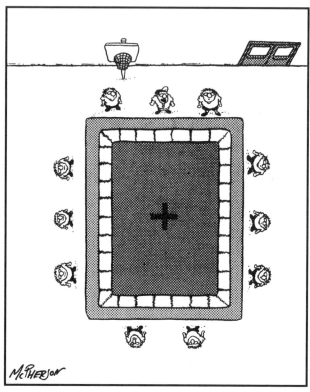

"Let go of the ceiling, Wilkins!"

The new converging conference room walls
helped to keep faculty meetings from
dragging on indefinitely.

Teaching kids to count is fine,
but teaching them what counts is best.

Bob Talbert

Every high school student's
worst enemy: the essay question.

Chuck's fascination with macrame
was beginning to annoy Coach Paparella.

In an incredible stroke of luck, Brian discovers
that the final "Jeopardy" question is the same
as the 20-point bonus question on his take-home midterm.

After constant complaints that she was assigning
too much homework, the administration ordered Mrs. Dernst
to walk the length of the school carrying all of her students' backpacks.

As the rash of lunchbag break-ins escalated,
many teachers in the faculty lounge began
to use The Lunch Club® to safeguard their food.

I have never let my schooling interfere with my education.

—Mark Twain

Mr. Gickman wasn't too good with names.

Although no one could quite put a finger on it,
there was something strangely
unnerving about the new biology teacher.

Vern messes up his right-turn signal again.

Striving to maintain her reputation as the school's most devious teacher, Mrs. Credley made her students write the 1,000-word final exam essay on the Invasion of Normandy using only candy Conversation Hearts.

"Well, at last we have a volunteer
to do the oral report on osmosis."

"I want to apologize to all of you for the side effects caused by last week's lab."

Inspired by the classic children's toy,
the new graduation caps helped students pass
the time during the lengthy commencement speeches.

"Bummer of a locker assignment, Walt."

"Man, did you scare me! For a second there
I thought you were my math teacher!"

Set design wasn't exactly a priority
with the Binkler High Drama Club.

"Ron, I'm your lab partner. Trust me."

High school goes high-tech with the onset of
the remote control locker opener.

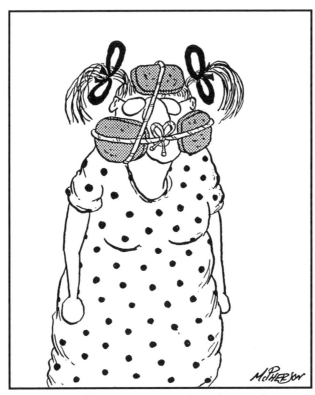

Louise Magnarski tests her theory that
cafeteria meatloaf can cure acne.

Education is learning what you didn't even know you didn't know.

Daniel J. Boorstin

After 17 years as a home ec. teacher,
Edwina Kratz was having a tough time
settling in as a chemistry teacher.

In a rare display of emotion, gym teacher
Art Mankowski succumbs to the spirit of Christmas.

Education is not a form of entertainment, but a means of empowering people to take control of their lives.

—Unknown

As a parting shot at her loathsome English teacher,
Jennifer Wrigley ended her valedictorian speech
with a dangling participle.

Wes Fumple had gotten downright lazy
when it came to taking notes.

As a service to mothers, school buses
at Douglasville School District were outfitted
with forgotten-item retrieval bins.

School librarian Nelda Limpkin was pretty pleased
with her new book classifying system.

"Mike made these for me in metal shop."

"I'll give you each a three-second head start, then I'll send Choonga up after you. If he catches you before you reach the top, you owe me 20 laps around the track."

Hoping to prevent students from running
in the halls, the school's new flypaper flooring
reduced accidents by 37 percent.

For a great practical joke, substitute some
Kool-Aid for your chemistry experiment, then drink it.

To encourage students to sit in the front row,
Varsteen High equipped all of its classrooms
with electronic massage recliners.

Although the new graduation process at
Burnsville High was faster, it didn't quite have
the glamour of the traditional graduation ceremony.

New for 2001: designer graduation caps.

*I am a teacher. A teacher is someone who leads.
There is no magic here. I do not walk on water.
I do not part the sea. I just love children.*

Marva Collins

In the midst of final exams, Noreen developed
an allergic reaction to algebra.

Professor Schnagle's exhilaration quickly faded
when he discovered that his secret new
hair-growing formula worked only on linoleum.

Physics students at Waterburg High School
attempt to measure the energy of a sneeze.

More and more students are turning
to private coaching firms to help them
score higher on the SAT.

Supporting Others

In the spirit and tradition of the *Chicken Soup for the Soul* series, we designate a charity to receive a portion of the net profits from each book. A portion of the proceeds from this book will be given to **The Horatio Alger Association of Distinguished Americans.**

The Horatio Alger Association of Distinguished Americans has honored the accomplishments and achievements of outstanding individuals in our society who have succeeded in the face of adversity since 1947. The Association encourages young people to pursue their dreams with determination and perseverance by bringing the "Horatio Alger Heroes" of today together with those of tomorrow by bestowing the Horatio Alger Award annually. This award bestows over $5 million in college scholarships and provides an internship and job placement program.

You may contact this organization at:

The Horatio Alger Association
99 Canal Center Plaza
Alexandria, VA 22314
phone: 703-684-9444 • fax: 703-548-3822
Web site: *www.horatioalger.com*

Who Is Jack Canfield?

Jack Canfield is one of America's leading experts in the development of human potential and personal effectiveness. He is both a dynamic, entertaining speaker and a highly sought-after trainer. Jack has a wonderful ability to inform and inspire audiences toward increased levels of self-esteem and peak performance.

He is the author and narrator of several bestselling audio- and videocassette programs, including *Self-Esteem and Peak Performance, How to Build High Self-Esteem, Self-Esteem in the Classroom* and *Chicken Soup for the Soul— Live*. He is regularly seen on television shows such as *Good Morning America, 20/20* and *NBC Nightly News*. Jack has coauthored numerous books, including the *Chicken Soup for the Soul* series, *Dare to Win* and *The Aladdin Factor* (all with Mark Victor Hansen), *100 Ways to Build Self-Concept in the Classroom* (with Harold C. Wells), *Heart at Work* (with Jacqueline Miller) and *The Power of Focus* (with Les Hewitt and Mark Victor Hansen).

For further information about Jack's books, tapes and training programs, or to schedule him for a presentation, please contact:

Jack Canfield
P.O. Box 30880
Santa Barbara, CA 93130
phone: 805-563-2935 • fax: 805-563-2945
Web site: *www.chickensoup.com*

Who Is Mark Victor Hansen?

Mark Victor Hansen is a professional speaker who in the last twenty years has made over 4,000 presentations to more than 2 million people in thirty-two countries. His presentations cover sales excellence and strategies; personal empowerment and development; and how to triple your income and double your time off.

Mark has spent a lifetime dedicated to his mission of making a profound and positive difference in people's lives. Throughout his career, he has inspired hundreds of thousands of people to create a more powerful and purposeful future for themselves while stimulating the sale of billions of dollars worth of goods and services.

Mark is a prolific writer and has authored *Future Diary, How to Achieve Total Prosperity* and *The Miracle of Tithing*. He is coauthor of the *Chicken Soup for the Soul* series, *Dare to Win* and *The Aladdin Factor* (all with Jack Canfield), *The Master Motivator* (with Joe Batten) and *The One Minute Millionaire* with Robert D. Allen.

For further information about Mark, write:

MVH & Associates
P.O. Box 7665
Newport Beach, CA 92658
phone: 949-759-9304 or 800-433-2314
fax: 949-722-6912
Web site: *www.chickensoup.com*

Who Is John McPherson?

John McPherson was raised in a faraway place called Painted Post, New York. (We're not making this up.) He began cartooning at the age of four, with the bulk of his work appearing on walls, furniture and, at one point, a neighbor's dog. Most of this early work was poorly received. Discouraged, John turned his creative efforts to Play-Doh, pipe cleaners and Spirograph.

For the next fifteen years, John put his cartooning career on hold, until one day, during a very dull college engineering class, John drew a doodle in his notebook. His career was reborn. From that point in 1983, John began to draw voraciously despite the fact that his cartoons looked like he had drawn them using a pencil taped to his nose.

In the years that followed, John's cartoons appeared regularly in over forty magazines, and in 1992 Universal Press Syndicate and John teamed up to launch *Close to Home*. Since that time, *Close to Home* has earned its way into 700 papers worldwide, including *The Washington Post, Los Angeles Times, Tokyo Times* and *Hanoi Daily News*. In addition, John has published numerous book collections of his work, a yearly block calendar and an award-winning line of greeting cards with Recycled Paper Products.

In addition to his cartooning, John is an active speaker, talking to groups about the rigors of syndicated cartooning. He can be reached at *closetohome@compuserve.com*.

John lives in Saratoga Springs, New York, with his wife and two boys. When not drawing cartoons or playing with his kids, John spends time expanding his collection of soda-can pull tabs.